CONTENTS

WELCOME TO THE WORLD OF INFOGRAPHICS

Using icons, graphics and pictograms, infographics visualise data and information in a whole new way!

MEASURE THE LENGTH OF THE BIGGEST PASSENGER SHIP IN FOOTBALL PITCHES

DISCOVER HOW MANY ELEPHANTS THIS TRUCK CAN CARRY

FIND OUT HOW AN ENORMOUS OCEAN LINER CAN FLOAT

SEE HOW THE HEIGHT OF A HUMAN COMPARES TO THESE GIANT ROCKETS

POWERFUL MACHINES

Even the toughest job can be made easier by using a simple machine, such as a lever or a pulley. They can also be combined to create complex and incredibly powerful machines and vehicles.

LEVERS

A lever uses a long bar and a pivot, or fulcrum, to move a load. Moving the pivot closer to the load means you need less effort to lift it. Levers are found in diggers and cranes.

LOAD = 2

EFFORT = 1

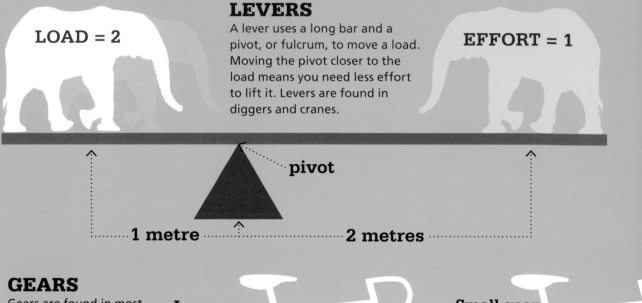

pivot

1 metre

2 metres

GEARS

Gears are found in most vehicles, including bicycles. They transmit force to the wheels. The larger the gear on the rear wheel of a bike, the smaller the amount the wheel will turn. Large gears make it easier to pedal up a hill.

Large gear

Small gear

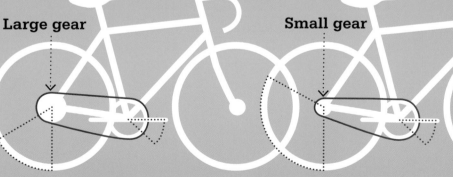

18

Large trucks have up to 18 gears to transmit power from their engines to the wheels so that the truck can pull a heavy load.

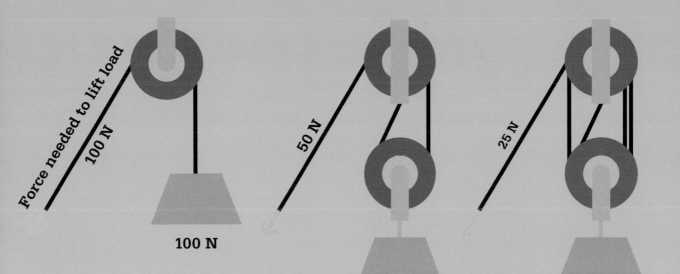

Force needed to lift load

100 N

100 N

50 N

100 N

25 N

100 N

PULLEYS

Pulleys are found on cranes and they use wheels and ropes to lift heavy objects. The more times a rope is fed through a pulley system, the easier it is to lift the load. Forces are measured in units called newtons (N).

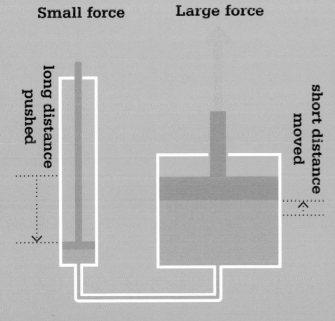

Small force

Large force

long distance pushed

short distance moved

20,000 TONNES

THE SAFE LIFTING CAPACITY OF THE WORLD'S STRONGEST CRANE. CALLED TAISUN, IT IS LOCATED IN THE YANTAI RAFFLES SHIPYARD IN CHINA.

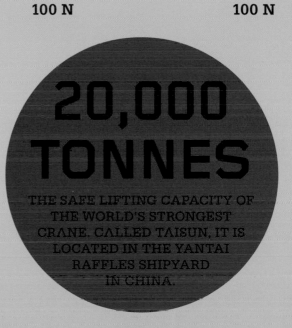

ATTRACT AND REPEL

Magnets will attract each other or repel each other depending on the orientation of their poles. This attracting and repelling can be used to pick up metal objects in a junkyard, or it can make a train hover above a magnetic track.

HYDRAULIC CYLINDERS

Hydraulics use liquids to transfer a force from one cylinder to another. A small force on a thin cylinder can create a large force on a thick cylinder. However, the force will only move the piston in the thick cylinder a short distance. Hydraulic cylinders are found on the arms of diggers or the hoppers of tipper trucks.

POWER UP!

Choosing the right energy source is vital to powering machines. The wind may be good enough to push a boat, but planes need a propeller or a powerful jet to fly, while space vehicles need a rocket.

PETROL CYCLE

The up-and-down action in a petrol engine cylinder is turned into a spinning movement by the crankshaft. Each time the crankshaft makes a complete circle is called a revolution. This type of engine is called an internal combustion engine, and they are found in cars, trucks and motorbikes.

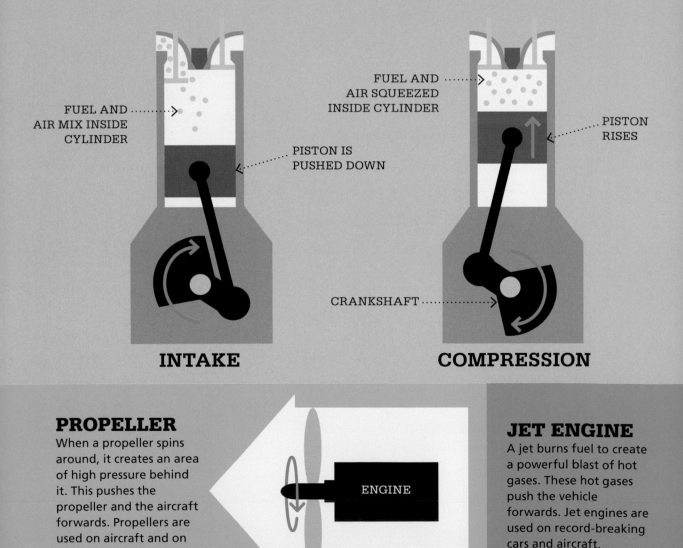

FUEL AND AIR MIX INSIDE CYLINDER

PISTON IS PUSHED DOWN

INTAKE

FUEL AND AIR SQUEEZED INSIDE CYLINDER

PISTON RISES

CRANKSHAFT

COMPRESSION

PROPELLER

When a propeller spins around, it creates an area of high pressure behind it. This pushes the propeller and the aircraft forwards. Propellers are used on aircraft and on powered boats and ships.

ENGINE

JET ENGINE

A jet burns fuel to create a powerful blast of hot gases. These hot gases push the vehicle forwards. Jet engines are used on record-breaking cars and aircraft.

WIND POWER

The wind is often harnessed to power machines. A yacht uses sails to catch the wind and push it forwards. To stop a yacht from being blown sideways it has a keel sticking down into the water.

SPINNAKER

WIND DIRECTION

MAINSAIL

KEEL

LIQUID OXYGEN

LIQUID FUEL

18,000

The maximum number of revolutions per minute in a Formula One engine.

EXHAUST GASES ARE PUSHED OUT

SPARK PLUG IGNITES FUEL AND AIR MIX

PISTON IS PUSHED DOWN

PISTON RISES

POWER

EXHAUST

OXYGEN AND FUEL ARE SET ALIGHT

HOT GASES PUSH THE ROCKET FORWARDS

ROCKETS

Rockets work by burning a fuel with a substance called an oxidiser. In most space rockets, both the fuel and the oxidiser are stored as liquids before being mixed together and ignited. Rockets are also found on very fast aircraft and fireworks.

FUEL BURNT IN COMBUSTION CHAMBER

AIR INTAKE

EXHAUST

7

ON THE MOVE

How people travel about and what they choose to travel in has changed a lot over time and varies greatly from one country to another. A bicycle may be ideal for a short trip, but a high-speed train or a super-fast jet are better for international journeys.

PERCENTAGE OF THE UK POPULATION WITH ACCESS TO A CAR

1951 **14%**

2008 **78%**

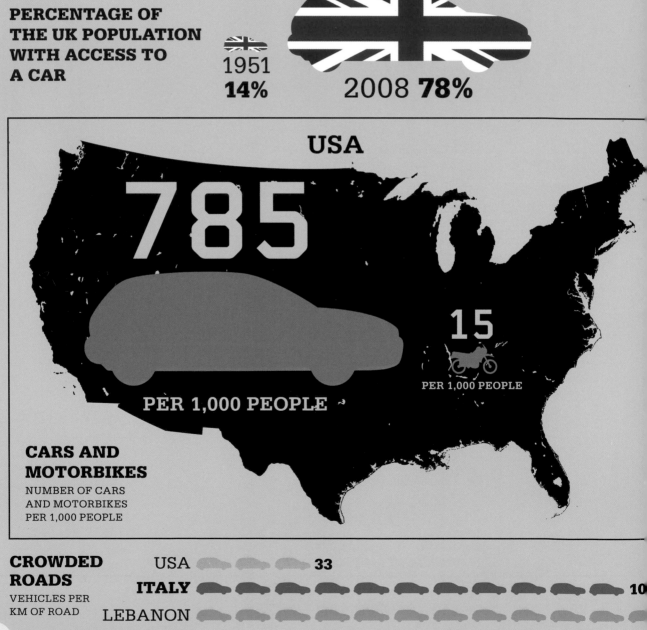

USA

785

15

PER 1,000 PEOPLE

PER 1,000 PEOPLE

CARS AND MOTORBIKES
NUMBER OF CARS AND MOTORBIKES PER 1,000 PEOPLE

CROWDED ROADS
VEHICLES PER KM OF ROAD

USA 33

ITALY 10

LEBANON

HONG KONG

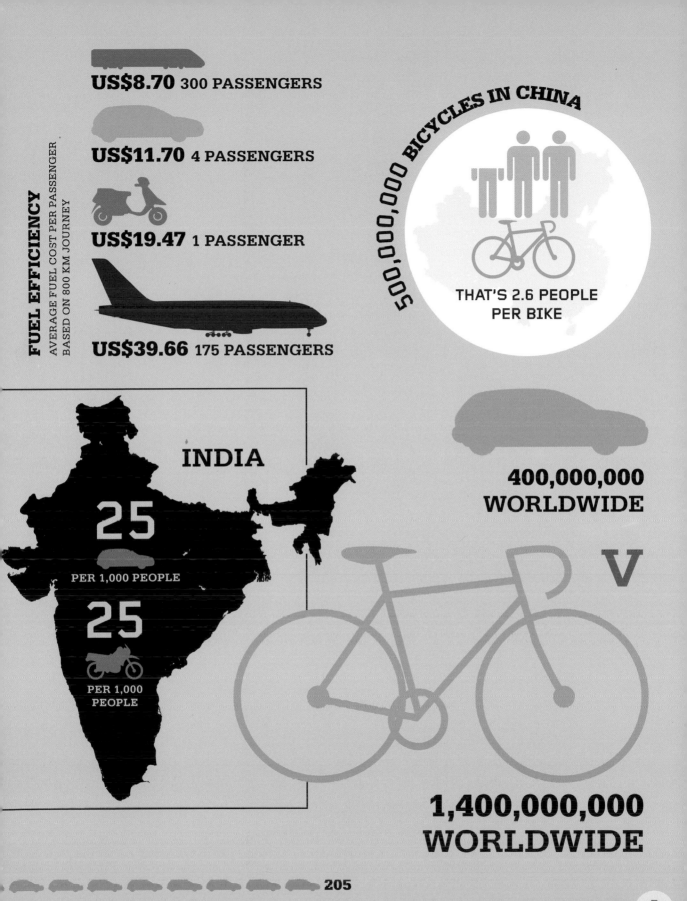

FUEL EFFICIENCY
AVERAGE FUEL COST PER PASSENGER BASED ON 800 KM JOURNEY

US$8.70 300 PASSENGERS

US$11.70 4 PASSENGERS

US$19.47 1 PASSENGER

US$39.66 175 PASSENGERS

500,000,000 BICYCLES IN CHINA

THAT'S 2.6 PEOPLE PER BIKE

400,000,000 WORLDWIDE

INDIA

25 PER 1,000 PEOPLE

25 PER 1,000 PEOPLE

V

1,400,000,000 WORLDWIDE

RECORD BREAKERS

Record-breaking machines are designed for one thing – to travel faster than anything else. They have special shapes that allow them to cut through the air or water as easily and as quickly as possible.

Record power

As well as a special shape, record breaking vehicles need a force to push them forwards. This force can come from a powerful jet engine, a roaring rocket or even the wind.

WATER SPEED RECORD
SPIRIT OF AUSTRALIA
511.11 KM/H

SAILING SPEED RECORD
HYDROPTÈRE
51.36 KNOTS

OLYMPIC SPRINTER
ABOUT 36 KM/H

THRUSTSSC (1997)
1,227.986 KM/H
ThrustSSC was fitted with two powerful jet fighter engines.

THRUST2 (1983)
1,019.47 KM/H

BLUE FLAME (1970)
1,001.667 KM/H

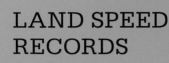

LAND SPEED RECORDS

88.8 The land speed record for a solar powered car stands at 88.8 km/h.

The shape of things

In order to move through the air or the water quickly, an object needs to be streamlined. A streamlined shape allows the air to flow around the vehicle easily. The more streamlined a vehicle is, the faster it can travel.

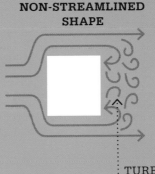

NON-STREAMLINED SHAPE

STREAMLINED SHAPE

AIR FLOW

TURBULENCE

LAND SPEED RECORD THRUSTSSC 1,227.986 KM/H

FLIGHT AIRSPEED RECORD LOCKHEED BLACKBIRD 3,529.6 KM/H

Formula One racing is at the cutting edge of car design. Modern Formula One cars use a specially designed shape and 'wings' to travel as quickly as possible around a racetrack.

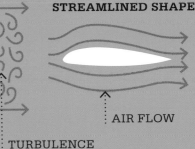

FORMULA ONE CAR **1950**

FORMULA ONE CAR **2012**

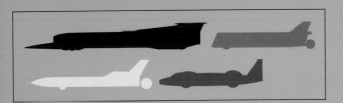

BLUEBIRD CN7 (1964) 644.96 KM/H

63.15

The first land speed record was set in 1898 at 63.15 km/h.

SLOWING DOWN

To slow down, vehicles need to use a force that works against their forward movement. To do this, they can either squeeze pads against their spinning wheels, deploy billowing parachutes behind them, or shoot out a powerful blast of gases.

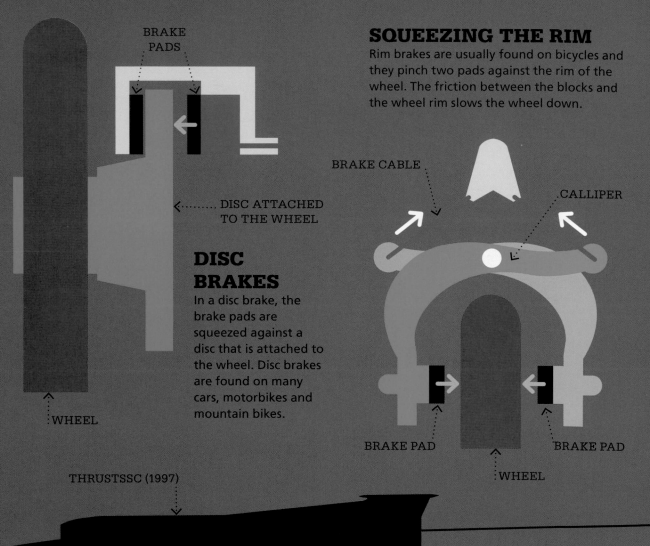

BRAKE PADS

DISC ATTACHED TO THE WHEEL

WHEEL

THRUSTSSC (1997)

DISC BRAKES

In a disc brake, the brake pads are squeezed against a disc that is attached to the wheel. Disc brakes are found on many cars, motorbikes and mountain bikes.

SQUEEZING THE RIM

Rim brakes are usually found on bicycles and they pinch two pads against the rim of the wheel. The friction between the blocks and the wheel rim slows the wheel down.

BRAKE CABLE

CALLIPER

BRAKE PAD

BRAKE PAD

WHEEL

12 METRES

The size of the parachute used to slow down a Space Shuttle after landing.

PARACHUTES

Parachutes work by increasing the air resistance, or drag, of an object as it moves. They are used to slow a person's fall from a plane or they are fitted to aircraft, drag racers and land speed record cars to slow them down.

DRUM BRAKES

Instead of pads, drum brakes push two curved 'shoes' against the inner surface of a drum that is attached to the wheel. This creates friction, which slows the drum and the wheel down. Drum brakes are fitted to cars and trucks.

BRAKE SHOE

BRAKE CABLE

BRAKE SHOE

DRUM

WHEEL

GOING RETRO

Retro rockets fire a blast of gases in the same direction as the movement in order to slow a vehicle down. Some space vehicles use retro rockets to slow down their descent to a planet's surface.

FORCE OF RETRO ROCKETS SLOWS DESCENT

The brakes on a **formula one** car can heat up to a temperature of **750°C** during a grand prix race.

THRUSTSSC BRAKING SYSTEM

ThrustSSC used a combination of disc brakes and two parachutes to slow it down. One small parachute was opened at 1,000 km/h to start the braking process. This was then released, and a second, larger parachute was opened once the car had slowed to 350 km/h.

PARACHUTE INCREASES AIR RESISTANCE TO SLOW DOWN THE VEHICLE

UP IN THE AIR

In order to soar into the sky, an aircraft can use specially shaped wings or it can make itself extra-light using heated air or special gases.

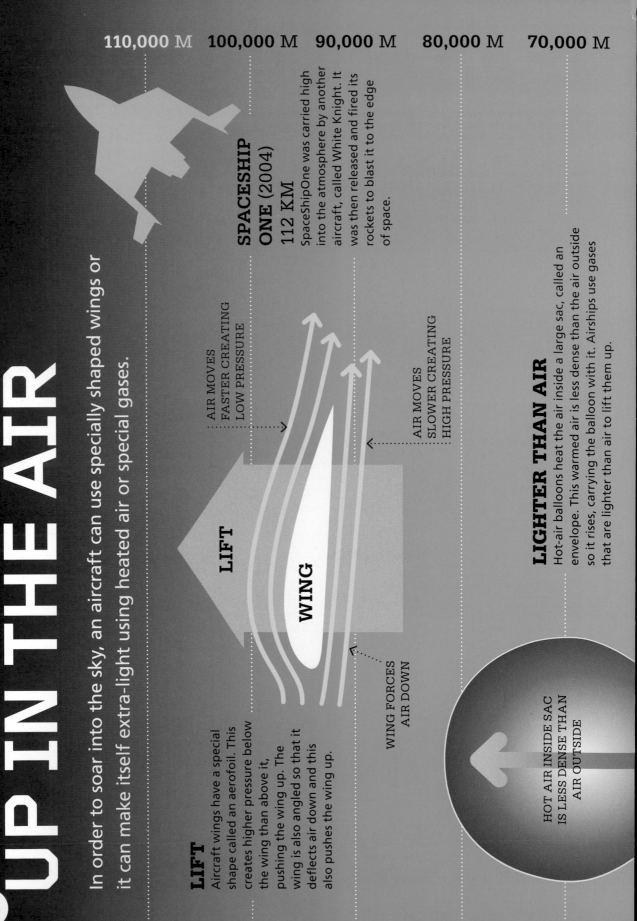

LIFT

Aircraft wings have a special shape called an aerofoil. This creates higher pressure below the wing than above it, pushing the wing up. The wing is also angled so that it deflects air down and this also pushes the wing up.

LIFT

WING

AIR MOVES FASTER CREATING LOW PRESSURE

AIR MOVES SLOWER CREATING HIGH PRESSURE

WING FORCES AIR DOWN

SPACESHIP ONE (2004) 112 KM

SpaceShipOne was carried high into the atmosphere by another aircraft, called White Knight. It was then released and fired its rockets to blast it to the edge of space.

LIGHTER THAN AIR

Hot-air balloons heat the air inside a large sac, called an envelope. This warmed air is less dense than the air outside so it rises, carrying the balloon with it. Airships use gases that are lighter than air to lift them up.

HOT AIR INSIDE SAC IS LESS DENSE THAN AIR OUTSIDE

AIRSHIP

AIR INSIDE BALLOON HEATED BY BURNERS

STRATO-LAB V (1961)
HIGHEST MANNED BALLOON
34,668 M
This balloon was filled with helium gas. It carried two people to a record-breaking altitude during a flight that lasted nine hours and 54 minutes.

MIG-25 (1977)
HIGHEST JET
37,650 M
As well as holding the record for the highest flying jet aircraft, the MiG-25 was also one of the fastest military jets, capable of flying at three times the speed of sound.

CONCORDE
CRUISING ALTITUDE
18,000 M
This passenger aircraft flew at more than twice the speed of sound. It could fly from London to New York in three and a half hours, whereas a standard passenger jet takes seven to eight hours.

HOT-AIR BALLOON (2004)
21,027 M
Vijaypat Singhania set the record for the highest hot-air balloon flight on 26 November 2005. His balloon was as tall as a 22-storey building.

MODERN PASSENGER JET
CRUISING ALTITUDE 10,000 M
Passenger airliners climb to a cruising altitude of around 10,000 m. At this height they are above any major turbulence caused by poor weather conditions closer to the ground.

FLYING GIANTS

Carrying heavy loads through the air needs some powerful flying machines. These giants use huge propellers, powerful jets or enormous bags of gas to get off the ground.

HEAVY LIFTING
MIL V-12
The world's largest helicopter was designed to lift 30,000 kg – that's about six elephants.

PASSENGER AIRSHIP
LZ 129 *HINDENBURG*
The *Hindenburg* was as tall as a 13-storey building, with a volume of 200,000 cubic metres – enough to fill 80 Olympic swimming pools.

CARGO AIRCRAFT
ANTONOV AN-225
The Antonov AN-225 is the world's heaviest aircraft. It has six powerful jet engines and a landing gear system with 32 wheels. It was designed to transport space rockets.

245 M
The overall length of the *Hindenburg*, longer than eight basketball courts.

1,600 M

The distance of the one and only flight performed by the Spruce Goose on 2 November 1947.

FLYING BOAT
HUGHES H-4
SPRUCE GOOSE

The Hughes H-4 Spruce Goose had a wingspan of 97.5 m, which is more than twice the length of the Wright Brothers' first powered flight (36.5 m).

PASSENGER JET **AIRBUS A380**

The Airbus A380 is 72.7 m long – as long as two blue whales. It has two passenger decks and can carry more than 500 people.

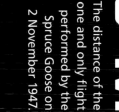

ON TRACK

Record-breaking trains need powerful locomotives to pull them along. Over the years, these super-fast locomotives have been powered by steam, electricity and even by magnets.

HIGH-SPEED TRAIN LINES

High-speed trains need special tracks that reduce the amount of vibration and do not have level crossings. These tracks allow the trains to travel at more than 200 km/h. Some countries, such as Japan, have a large high-speed line network.

FRANCE 1,872 KM

GERMANY 1,285 KM

UK 113 KM

JAPAN 2,452 KM

USA 362 KM

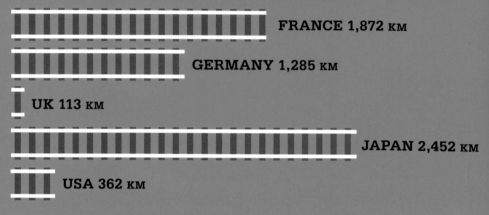

TGV
574.8 KM/H
Short for *Train à Grande Vitesse* (meaning 'high-speed train'), a test model of this electric-powered French locomotive set the record for the fastest wheeled train, reaching 574.8 km/h on 3 April 2007.

JR-MAGLEV
581 KM/H
The Japanese JR-Maglev set a record speed for a tracked vehicle of 581 km/h on 2 December 2003.

LONGEST TRAIN BHP FREIGHT TRAIN
21 JUNE 2001, WESTERN AUSTRALIA

683 WAGONS, **8** LOCOMOTIVES **7.353** KM LONG **99,700** TONNES

The world's **earliest** railway dates from the **sixth century BC**. The Diolkos wagonway in Greece was just **6 km** long.

STEPHENSON'S *ROCKET* ⋯⋯>
48 KM/H

The *Rocket* was built in 1829 to take part in the Rainhill Trials. These were tests to see which type of locomotive would work on one of the first train lines – the *Rocket* won.

MALLARD ⋯⋯>
202.6 KM/H

Built in 1938, the *Mallard* still holds the record for the world's fastest steam-powered locomotive.

1,139,615 KM

The total amount of railtrack in the entire world. The USA has 224,792 km of railtrack, Russia has 87,157 km and China has about 86,00 km.

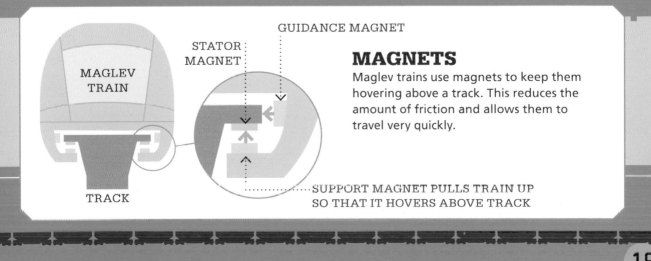

GUIDANCE MAGNET

STATOR MAGNET

MAGLEV TRAIN

TRACK

MAGNETS

Maglev trains use magnets to keep them hovering above a track. This reduces the amount of friction and allows them to travel very quickly.

SUPPORT MAGNET PULLS TRAIN UP SO THAT IT HOVERS ABOVE TRACK

WATER WORLD

Gigantic ocean-going ships are used to carry military aircraft, huge amounts of crude oil or thousands of passengers on a holiday cruise. They are some of the largest machines on the planet.

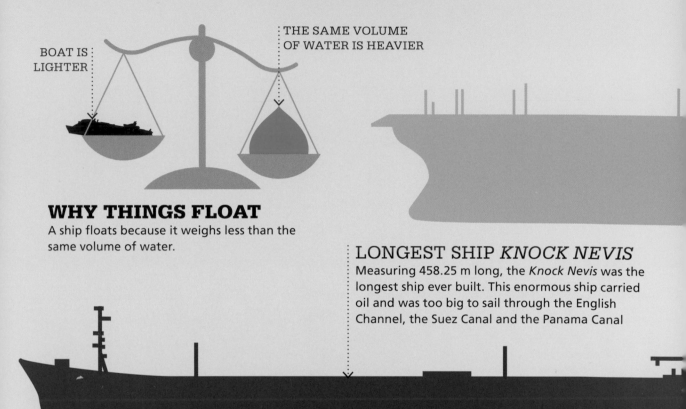

BOAT IS LIGHTER

THE SAME VOLUME OF WATER IS HEAVIER

WHY THINGS FLOAT
A ship floats because it weighs less than the same volume of water.

LONGEST SHIP *KNOCK NEVIS*
Measuring 458.25 m long, the *Knock Nevis* was the longest ship ever built. This enormous ship carried oil and was too big to sail through the English Channel, the Suez Canal and the Panama Canal

PASSENGER SHIP *OASIS OF THE SEAS*
This enormous liner contains a casino, mini golf course, nightclubs and volleyball and basketball courts.

Oasis of the Seas has enough electrical cable to stretch between London and New York.

FIVE TIMES BIGGER THAN THE *TITANIC*

BIGGEST PROPELLER

The world's largest propeller has a mass of

130 TONNES.

This six-bladed monster is used to power the *Emma Maersk*, the biggest container ship on the planet. The propeller can push this massive ship and its load of nearly 15,000 containers at a cruising speed of 27 knots (50 km/h).

9.6 M

NAVAL VESSEL
USS *ENTERPRISE*

This aircraft carrier is the longest naval vessel in the world. It is 342 m long and has a crew of nearly 6,000, including 1,800 pilots and aircrew.

TONNAGE 225,282
LENGTH 360 M
HEIGHT 72 M ABOVE WATER LINE
DECKS 16 PASSENGER DECKS
SPEED 22.6 KNOTS (41.9 KM/H)
CAPACITY 6,296 MAXIMUM **CREW** 2,165

FIVE

The number of swimming pools on board the *Oasis of the Seas*.

LONGER THAN THREE FOOTBALL PITCHES

BENEATH THE WAVES

Deep beneath the surface of the ocean, water pressures are so great that they could squash a person flat. Vehicles that can dive to these depths are specially designed to withstand these forces.

1,000 M **2,000 M** **3,000 M** **4,000 M**

FREE DIVING 273 M

SCUBA DIVING 330 M

ATMOSPHERIC DIVING SUIT 610 M

MILITARY SUBMARINE 1,300 M

COLOSSAL SQUID 2,200 M

SPERM WHALE 3,000 M

WRECK OF *TITANIC* 3,780 M

The wreck of the *Titanic* was found in September 1985. It lies in two pieces with debris scattered over 5 square kilometres

DIVING AND SURFACING

Submarines dive and rise in the water by altering their buoyancy. This is their ability to float. They alter their buoyancy by pumping air and water into and out of special tanks.

AIR PUMPED INTO TANKS

RISING

WATER PUMPED OUT

AIR PUMPED OUT OF TANKS

DIVING

WATER PUMPED IN

1620

The first-ever submarine was built by Cornelius van Drebbel around 1620 and travelled below the surface of the Thames to depths of 5 metres.

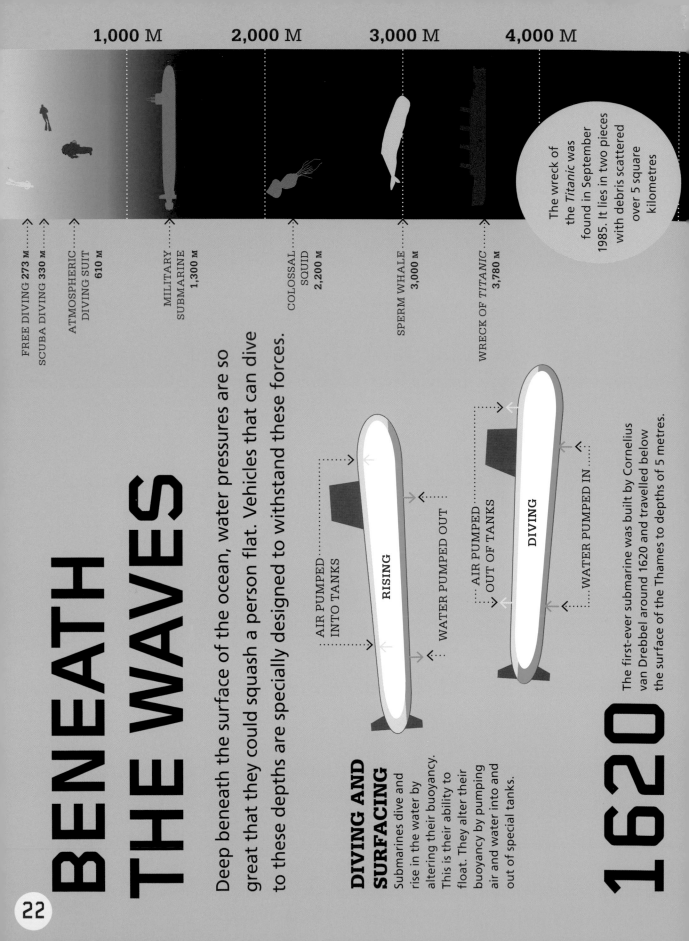

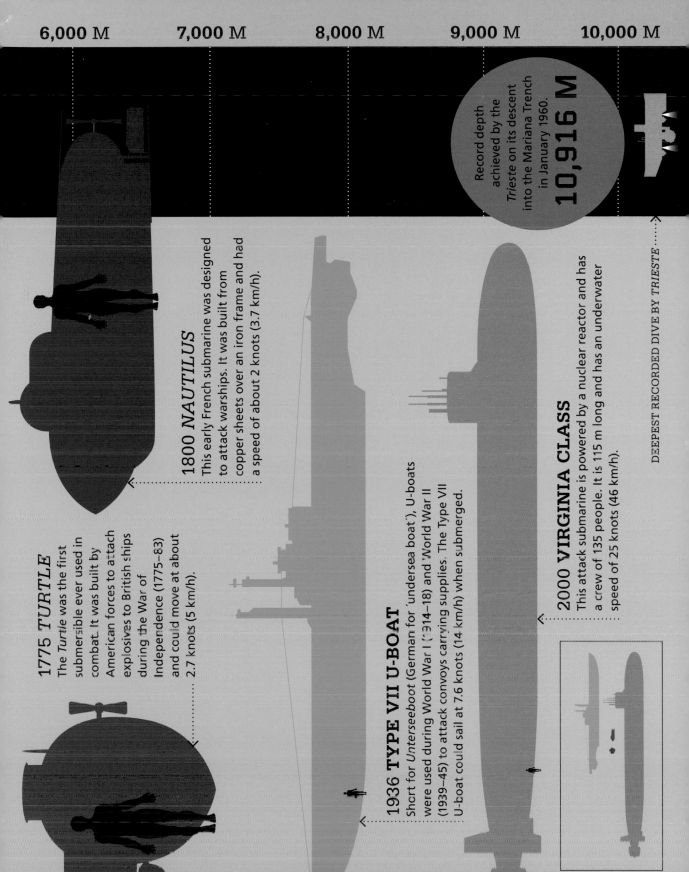

Record depth achieved by the *Trieste* on its descent into the Mariana Trench in January 1960. **10,916 M**

DEEPEST RECORDED DIVE BY *TRIESTE*

1800 *NAUTILUS*
This early French submarine was designed to attack warships. It was built from copper sheets over an iron frame and had a speed of about 2 knots (3.7 km/h).

1775 *TURTLE*
The *Turtle* was the first submersible ever used in combat. It was built by American forces to attach explosives to British ships during the War of Independence (1775–83) and could move at about 2.7 knots (5 km/h).

1936 **TYPE VII U-BOAT**
Short for *Unterseeboot* (German for 'undersea boat'), U-boats were used during World War I (1914–18) and World War II (1939–45) to attack convoys carrying supplies. The Type VII U-boat could sail at 7.6 knots (14 km/h) when submerged.

2000 **VIRGINIA CLASS**
This attack submarine is powered by a nuclear reactor and has a crew of 135 people. It is 115 m long and has an underwater speed of 25 knots (46 km/h).

MONSTER MACHINES

Industrial vehicles are designed to move massive loads from one place to another. This could be earth and rubble, petrol or even space rockets. Whatever they carry, these vehicles are designed to be big enough and powerful enough to handle huge weights.

BIGGEST TIPPER TRUCK
LIEBHERR T 282B

This massive truck is designed to carry a load of more than 350 tonnes – that is nearly 70 elephants! It uses hydraulics (see page 7) to push its hopper up to empty a load.

WORLD'S LARGEST MOVEABLE INDUSTRIAL MACHINE

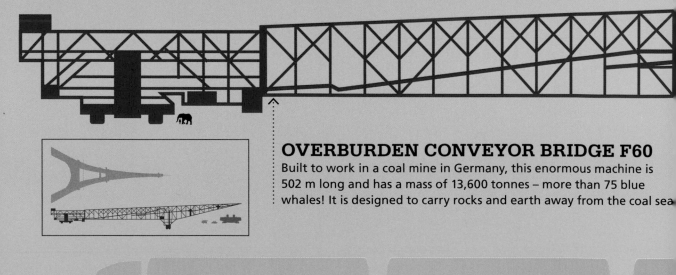

OVERBURDEN CONVEYOR BRIDGE F60

Built to work in a coal mine in Germany, this enormous machine is 502 m long and has a mass of 13,600 tonnes – more than 75 blue whales! It is designed to carry rocks and earth away from the coal sea

BIGGEST BULLDOZER
D575A-3SD

This monster machine is fitted with a huge blade on the front that can push 96 cubic metres of earth and rubble at a time.

14.91 M

The height of the Leibherr T 282B when the hopper is raised to its maximum.

MOBILE LAUNCH PLATFORM

Built to transport the massive Saturn V rockets (see pages 28–29), this giant measures 49 m by 41 m. When it carried an unfuelled Space Shuttle, it had a mass of 5,000 tonnes.

ROAD TRAIN
MACK TITAN

The world's longest road train to be pulled by a single unit measured 1,474.3 m long. It consisted of 112 trailers and had a mass of 1,300 tonnes and was driven just 100 m on 18 February 2006.

50,000 TONNES

The amount of material the Overburden Corveyor Bridge F60 can move in an hour. That is enough to cover a football pitch to a depth of up to 8 m.

DIGGING DEEP

These digging machines use claw-like shovels, enormous spinning wheels or rotating discs covered in sharp teeth to cut, slice and tear through rock and earth.

LARGEST HYDRAULIC SHOVEL
TEREX RH400

Moved by a powerful hydraulics system (see page 7), the enormous shovel on this excavator can lift 86 tonnes of rubble – that is 17 elephants.

LARGEST LAND VEHICLE
BAGGER 288

Used in a coal mine in Germany, this machine can fill 2,400 coal wagons in a single day. It is 220 m long.

The enormous digging wheel measures 21.6 m across and has 18 huge buckets.

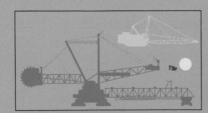

Big Muskie needed a round-the-clock crew of five to run it and it used as much energy to power it as 27,500 homes.

<------------ BUCKET

LARGEST DRAGLINE EXCAVATOR
BIG MUSKIE

This excavator used pulleys and levers (see pages 6–7) to move its enormous bucket, which was big enough to fit two single-decker buses. It operated at a mine in the USA from 1969 until 1991.

30 M

The depth of earth the Bagger 288 could cover a football pitch with in a single day.

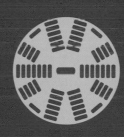

TUNNEL BORING MACHINE

The largest tunnel boring machine designed to cut through hard rock measured 14.4 m across. It was used to dig a tunnel beneath Niagara Falls, Canada, as part of a hydroelectric power station.

96 M
The height of the Bagger 288 – as tall as a 25-storey building.

BLAST OFF!

Rockets are used to power vehicles to incredible speeds. They are the only energy source that can push a vehicle high into the atmosphere and even out into space.

IN STAGES

Many space rockets come in parts, known as stages. Each stage has its own rocket engines and fuel supply. When a stage has run out of fuel, it is ejected, making the whole rocket lighter. The engines on the next stage ignite and the rocket climbs higher.

3. UPPER STAGE IGNITES ROCKET AND RELEASES LOWER STAGE.

2. ROCKET BOOSTERS RELEASED HIGH IN THE ATMOSPHERE.

1. ROCKET BLASTS OFF WITH BOOSTERS STRAPPED TO ITS SIDES.

ZERO GRAVITY AT MAXIMUM HEIGHT

RE-ENTRY WITH FOLDED WINGS

90-SECOND CLIMB AT 4,000 KM/H

UNPOWERED GLIDE

SPACESHIPTWO AND CARRIER AIRCRAFT SEPARATE

SPACE PLANE

SpaceShipTwo is designed to be carried high into the atmosphere by another aircraft before it is released. It then ignites its rockets to blast to the edge of space, before gliding back down to land.

SATURN V USA

The mighty Saturn V holds the records for being the tallest and heaviest rocket ever built and for delivering the heaviest payload. Thirteen of these giants were launched, carrying people to the Moon and space stations into orbit.

SPACE SHUTTLE USA

Used to launch satellites and space probes from 1981 to 2011, Space Shuttles were reusable. They were strapped to enormous fuel tanks and powerful boosters, which were released high in the atmosphere.

ARIANNE 5 EUROPE

This rocket has two powerful boosters strapped to its sides, as well as a main engine. It releases these boosters when they have used up all of their fuel.

VOSTOK USSR

The Vostok rockets were developed from long-range missiles. The first artificial satellite, Sputnik, was launched into orbit by one of these rockets.

MERCURY USA

The Mercury space program was the first successful American attempt to send people into space. Mercury capsules were launched on top of Atlas rockets.

V2 GERMANY

This long-range missile was developed by Germany during World War II. It was designed to blast high into the atmosphere and had a range of 320 km.

THE LARGEST ROCKET EVER BUILT IS THE SATURN V – IT WAS 110.6 M TALL.

GLOSSARY

aerofoil
The special shape of a wing, which produces higher pressure below than above, creating a pushing force. This force can lift an aircraft into the air or push a racing car down into the track to improve its grip.

attract
When an object pulls something towards itself. Opposite magnetic poles on two magnets will be attracted to each other.

buoyancy
The ability of a ship or boat to float in water. A ship will float if it weighs less than the same volume of water.

compression
When something is squeezed together.

friction
The force produced when two objects or materials rub together. Rough objects produce more friction, making them harder to move, while smooth objects produce less friction.

fulcrum
The point around which a lever works. It is also known as the pivot.

gears
Wheels or bars with teeth that interlock with the teeth on other wheels or a chain. They are used to transmit a force.

hydraulics
A system that uses a liquid to transmit a force. Squeezing the liquid at one end will produce a pushing force at the other end of the system. The size of the force can be adjusted by altering the size of the cylinders and pistons.

hydroelectric power station
A power station that uses the movement of water to produce electricity. This water is usually stored in a large, artificial lake.

internal combustion
The process of producing a driving force by burning a fuel inside a cylinder. This explosion pushes a piston down and this motion can be used to move a vehicle or power machinery.

locomotive
The powered vehicle that is used to move a train. Locomotives can be driven by steam, internal combustion engines, electric motors or magnets.

knot
A unit of speed used to measure the movement of ships and boats. It stands for 'nautical miles per hour'.

lever
A long bar that moves around a pivot, or fulcrum, to transmit a force. Levers are usually used to move or lift an object.

payload
The cargo carried by an aircraft or rocket, which earns money. A rocket's payload can include a satellite, a space probe or a fee-paying astronaut.

pole
One of the two ends of a magnet. A magnetic pole can be either North (N) or South (S).

repel
When an object pushes something away from itself. If two magnetic poles that are the same are put close to each other, they will repel and push each other away.

range
The distance an object or vehicle can travel. The range of a vehicle is usually the distance it can travel without having to refuel.

streamlined
An object that is streamlined is able to move through the air or through water as easily as possible.

turbulence
The swirling, irregular movement of a gas or liquid. Turbulence created by a non-streamlined car, for example, will increase the force called drag, making it harder for the car to move and slowing it down.

pulleys
A simple machine that uses a system of ropes and wheels to move an object. The more times the rope passes through the system, the easier it is to move the object.

Websites

MORE INFO:
airandspace.si.edu
Website of the Smithsonian Institute's Air and Space Museum. It contains details of exhibitions at the museum as well as teaching resources and online activities.

www.sciencemuseum.org.uk
Home page of the Science Museum, it features online material, including teacher resources, descriptions of exhibits, games and explanations.

www.howstuffworks.com
A massive website featuring explanations of how nearly everything works, including machines and vehicles. It features videos, games and blogs.

MORE GRAPHICS:
www.visualinformation.info
A website that contains a whole host of infographic material on subjects as diverse as natural history, science, sport and computer games.

www.coolinfographics.com
A collection of infographics and data visualisations from other online resources, magazines and newspapers

www.dailyinfographic.com
A comprehensive collection of infographics on an enormous range of topics that is updated every single day!

INDEX

ACKNOWLEDGEMENTS

Published in paperback in 2014 by Wayland
Copyright © Wayland 2014

Wayland
338 Euston Road
London NW1 3BH

Wayland Australia
Level 17/207 Kent Street
Sydney NSW 2000

All rights reserved.
Senior editor: Julia Adams

Produced by Tall Tree Ltd

Editor: Jon Richards
Designer: Ed Simkins
Consultant: Penny Johnson

British Library Cataloguing in Publication Data
Richards, Jon, 1970-
  The world in infographics.
  Machines and vehicles.
  1. Machinery--Charts, diagrams, etc.--Juvenile
  literature. 2. Vehicles--Charts, diagrams,
  etc.--Juvenile literature.
  I. Title II. Machines and vehicles III. Simkins, Ed.
  621.8-dc23
  ISBN: 9780750281287
Printed in Malaysia

10 9 8 7 6 5 4 3 2 1
Wayland is a division of Hachette
Children's Books, an Hachette UK company.
www.hachette.co.uk

The website addresses (URLs) included in this
book were valid at the time of going to press.
However, because of the nature of the Internet,
it is possible that some addresses may have
changed, or sites may have changed or closed
down, since publication. While the author and
Publisher regret any inconvenience this may
cause the readers, no responsibility for any such
changes can be accepted by either the author
or the Publisher.